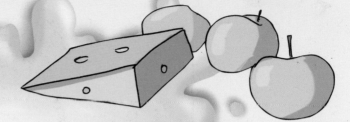

CURIOUS PEARL

SCIENCE GIRL

CURIOUS PEARL EXPLAINS STATES OF MATTER

by Eric Braun

illustrated by Stephanie Dehennin

raintree

a Capstone company — publishers for children

Curious Pearl here! Do you like science? I certainly do! I have all sorts of fun tools to help me observe and investigate, but my favourite tool is my science notebook. That's where I write down questions and facts that help me learn more about science. Would you like to join me on my science adventures? You're in for a special surprise!

Download the Capstone 4D app!

Videos for all of the notebook features in this book are at your fingertips with the 4D app.

To download the Capstone 4D app:
- Search in the Apple App Store or Google Play for "Capstone 4D"
- Click Install (Android) or Get, then Install (Apple)
- Open the application
- Scan any page with this icon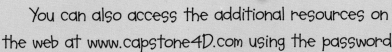

You can also access the additional resources on the web at www.capstone4D.com using the password

pearl.matter

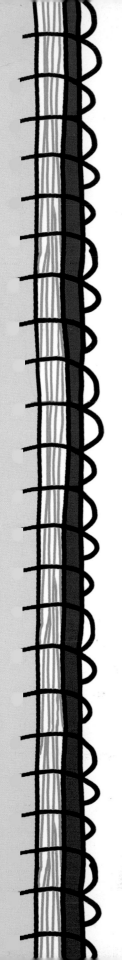

Summer is the best season, isn't it? There is lots of time for playing and riding my bike. I get to play with my little brother, Peter, too.

Peter likes summer as much as I do. And Peter loves ice lollies. He loves them like the sky loves the stars. Like I love science!

Today Peter and I were playing outside with our friends. Suddenly, Peter screamed, "We need ice lollies!"

"That sounds serious!" I told my friends. "I'd better find some ice lollies."

I went inside to find an ice lolly. But we didn't have any. I grabbed some cheese and crackers. I also got apples and peanut butter.

"Ice lollies! Ice lollies!" he cried.

"All right," I said. "Let's make some ice lollies out of juice."

"We can't turn juice into an ice lolly!" Peter said.

"Of course we can," I said. "It's just a matter of MATTER."

"What is the matter?" he asked.

"Nothing is the matter," I said. "But everything is MATTER. Juice, ice lollies, air, chairs and even people are made of matter."

"Wait," Peter said. "Air? Air isn't made of anything."

"Yes, even air! It's a gas. Gas is one state of matter. Liquid is another state – like this orange juice. The other state is solid. This worktop is a solid."

I knocked my knuckles on it. "And so are ice lollies."

Peter shook his head. "I still don't get how air is matter," he said.

I was about to explain it to him. But then I realized I didn't really get it either.

"Let's see what we can observe about these states of matter," I said.

"Well, if air is matter, it doesn't have any shape," Peter said.

"Eureka! That's true!" I said. Eureka is a scientific word. I use it when I make a new discovery.

I pulled out my trusty science notebook and pencil.

Gas, like air, has no shape. You can move through it.

"Compare that to liquid," I said.

"Liquid just sort of sloshes and changes shape," Peter said. "If we poured it on the floor, it would be flat like the floor too."

"Please don't pour it on the floor," I said. You never know what little brothers will do!

"The orange juice in the ice lolly mould is shaped like the mould," I noted.

Peter stuck his finger into one of the moulds. "And you can poke your finger into it," he said.

I wrote about liquids in my science notebook.

Liquid changes shape to fit its container. Like air, things can move through liquid.

"Are the ice lollies ready to go in the freezer yet?"
Peter asked.

"Yes," I said. "But first, tell me what you observe
about solids."

"Solids are solid!" he said, grinning.

"Eureka! That's true!" I said. "But what does
that mean?"

Peter patted the worktop, testing it. He tapped his foot on the floor – another solid. He picked up the ice lolly moulds and felt them.

"I think solid means it has its own shape, and you can't change it," he said.

"Good thinking!" I replied.

I was about to make a note in my notebook.
But just then, Peter dropped the ice lolly moulds.
Orange juice splattered all over the place! And
guess what else? One of the moulds broke in half.

"So you *can* change a solid's shape," I said.

Solids do not change shape to fit a container. But you can break, carve or sculpt them to change their shape.

You can't move through a solid.

I helped Peter clean up the mess. Then we poured orange juice into another set of ice lolly moulds. We put the moulds into the freezer.

"They will take some time to freeze," I told Peter. "Let's eat lunch while we wait." I took out a box of cheesy macaroni. Next, I poured water into a pan. Then I found Mum to help me turn on the stove.

Peter said, "One time, I lost an ice lolly in bed."

"Yuck!" I replied.

"Yeah," he said. "When I found it again, it had melted. So a solid can become a liquid. But when does that happen, exactly?"

"Eureka! Good observation!" I said. "Liquids freeze at freezing point. When water freezes, it becomes a solid – ice. Water's freezing point is 0 degrees Celsius (32 degrees Fahrenheit). That's also its melting point. So if the temperature of ice goes above 0 degrees C (32 degrees F), it will turn into a liquid."

"What about gas?" Peter asked. "Can anything turn into a gas?"

"Look!" I said. I pointed to the water boiling on the cooker. Steam was rising from the pan. "Liquid turns into a gas at its boiling point. Water's boiling point is 100 degrees C (212 degrees F)."

Time for another note in my science notebook!

Matter changes state when its temperature changes enough.

"Even the ice lolly moulds would become a liquid if they got hot enough," I said.

"But I still don't get how air is supposed to be matter," Peter said. "It's like nothing."

After lunch, Peter and I searched online. We learned about atoms. All matter is made up of atoms. The state of any matter changes, depending on how close together the atoms are.

"Huh?" Peter said.

"I'll show you," I said.

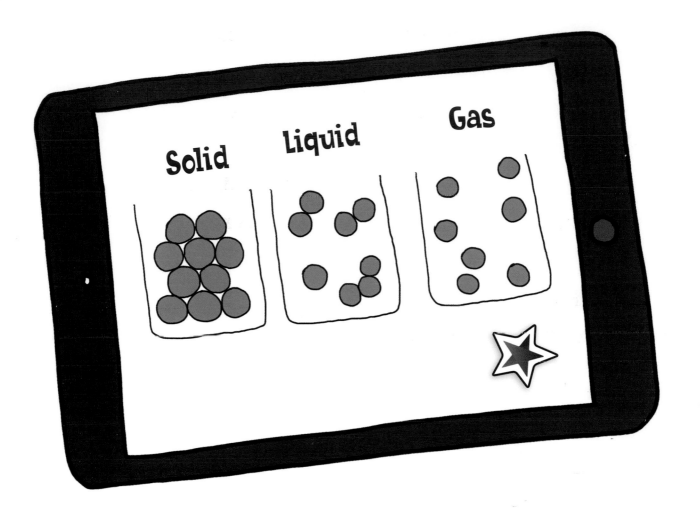

I explained the drawings to Peter. "Atoms in a solid are very close together. They can't move, and you can't get through them. In a liquid, the atoms are further apart. They can move a little bit. The atoms in a gas are even further apart. It's easy to pass through a gas like air or steam."

"Pearl?" Peter asked.

"Yes?" I said. I tried to imagine the next science question he might ask. I was ready to answer it!

"Are the ice lollies ready?" he asked.

Well, that's an easy question to answer. I opened the freezer and checked. They were ready! Peter and I took ice lollies to our friends outside.

"You know," Peter said, licking his lips. "I like science!"

SCIENCE ACTIVITY

If you like frozen treats, you can make ice lollies like Pearl and Peter did. Or you can even make ice cream! This is a fun way to see liquid change into a solid.

What you need:

115 ml full-fat milk

115 ml cream

60 g white sugar

½ teaspoon vanilla extract

120 g table salt or rock salt

260 g ice cubes

1 sandwich bag with zipper

1 large bag with zipper

What you do:

1. Pour the milk, cream, sugar and vanilla into the small bag. Zip it up tight so it doesn't leak!

2. Put the ice cubes and salt into the large bag.

3. Put the smaller bag inside the large bag along with the ice and salt. Seal the bag.

4. Hold the bag by the zipper at the top, and shake it. Keep shaking it until the ingredients in the small bag are solid. This will take about 10 minutes.

5. Remove the smaller bag from the bigger one, and serve your ice cream!

If you like, you can add your extra treats into the mixture before you shake the ice cream. But doing that will make the ice cream take longer to freeze. You can also put your extras on top after serving.

GLOSSARY

freeze become a solid or icy at a very low temperature

gas form of matter that is not solid or liquid; it can move about freely and does not have a definite shape

liquid form of matter that is wet and can be poured and takes the shape if its container

matter anything that has weight and takes up space, such as a gas, a liquid or a solid

melt change from a solid to a liquid; ice or snow melts above 0 degrees Celsius (32 degrees Fahrenheit)

observe watch someone or something closely in order to learn something

particle extremely tiny piece of matter; particles are too small to be seen with the naked eye

solid form of matter that does not easily change shape and can't be passed through

BOOKS

Experiments in Material and Matter with Toys and Everyday Stuff (Fun Science), Natalie Rompella (Raintree, 2016)

Matter (Moving Up With Science), Peter Riley (Franklin Watts, 2016)

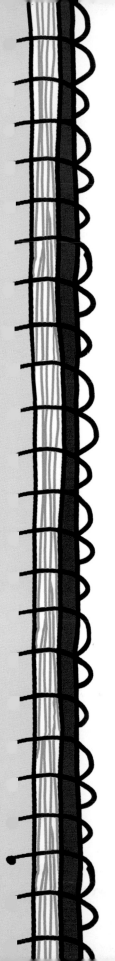

WEBSITES

www.bbc.co.uk/education/topics/zkgg87h
This website includes more information about solids, liquids and gases.

www.dkfindout.com/uk/science/solids-liquids- and-gases
Find out more about solids, liquids and gases.

COMPREHENSION QUESTIONS

When have you seen matter change states? Name as many examples as you can.

Have you ever seen dew on grass or plants in the morning? Where do you think it comes from?

Can you think of a way to get the salt out of salt water? Explain your idea.

MORE BOOKS IN THE SERIES

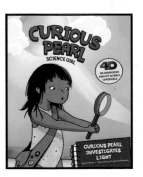

INDEX

Raintree is an imprint of Capstone Global Library Limited, a company incorporated in England and Wales having its registered office at 264 Banbury Road, Oxford, OX2 7DY – Registered company number: 6695582

www.raintree.co.uk
myorders@raintree.co.uk

Text © Capstone Global Library Limited 2018
The moral rights of the proprietor have been asserted.

Edited by Shelly Lyons
Designed by Ted Williams
Art Director: Nathan Gassman
Production by Katy LaVigne
Printed and bound in China

ISBN 978 1 4747 4050 0
21 20 19 18 17
10 9 8 7 6 5 4 3 2 1

British Library Cataloguing in Publication Data
A full catalogue record for this book is available from the British Library.

Acknowledgements
We would like to thank Christopher T Ruhland, PhD, for his invaluable help in the preparation of this book.

The illustrations in this book were digitally produced.

Every effort has been made to contact copyright holders of material reproduced in this book. Any omissions will be rectified in subsequent printings if notice is given to the publisher.

All the Internet addresses (URLs) given in this book were valid at the time of going to press. However, due to the dynamic nature of the Internet, some addresses may have changed, or sites may have changed or ceased to exist since publication. While the author and publisher regret any inconvenience this may cause readers, no responsibility for any such changes can be accepted by either the author or the publisher.